Casey Goes To
Washington

"The Washington, Lincoln, & Jefferson Memorial Tour"

Casey Jacobs

Written by Casey Jacobs
Selected Photographs by Andrew Linden

Text copyright © 2005 Casey Jacobs
Selected photographs copyright © 2005 Andrew Linden

Published in the United States of America
By Promise Publishing
P.O. Box 2221
Reston, Virginia 20195

Library of Congress Data

LCCN 2005922171

1. Washington DC – tour guide.
2. Washington Monuments – Nonfiction.
3. Children's

Jacobs, Casey.

Casey Goes to Washington by Casey Jacobs. Selected photographs by Andrew Linden.
Design by Jerel Motos, Farhan Shahzad, and Paul Reid.

Summary: Casey, a young boy living in the Washington DC area, shares his wealth of knowledge by giving readers a tour of the Nation's Capital – from a child's perspective. For more information, please visit **www.CaseyBooks.com**

ISBN 0-9766440-0-2

Quality discounts are available on bulk purchases of this book for educational, gift purposes, or as premiums for increasing magazine subscriptions or renewals.
Contact: Promise Publishing, ph 703-965-3715

Printed in the United States of America

 # CONTENTS

This book is dedicated to my Grandpa Casey —
a special tour guide.

Meet my friends in this book:

Niko, you've been a cool and close friend since we were three years old.
Dillon, you're an awesome classmate.
Emily, you're a special and kind friend. I like skating with you.
Janay, thank you for being a good friend.
Connor, you're a good brother. I love you.

Andy, I think you are the best photographer ever.

To my mom and dad, thank you for helping me with my book.

Hi, my name's Casey and I'll be your tour guide. Washington DC is a fun and busy place to visit. It's over 200 years old and has so much to see. So, put on your jacket and comfortable shoes, and let's take a walk.

Casey

"Look UP!"

The Washington
Monument

...is our first stop today. It was named after America's first president, George Washington. He died in 1799. And in 1833, citizens began raising money to build a memorial for him. In 1854, people started arguing and the construction stopped. Over twenty years later, Congress decided to get the monument finished. And lucky for you, this building was finally opened to the public in 1888.

This is the Reflecting Pool that separates the National Mall.
Don't fall in!

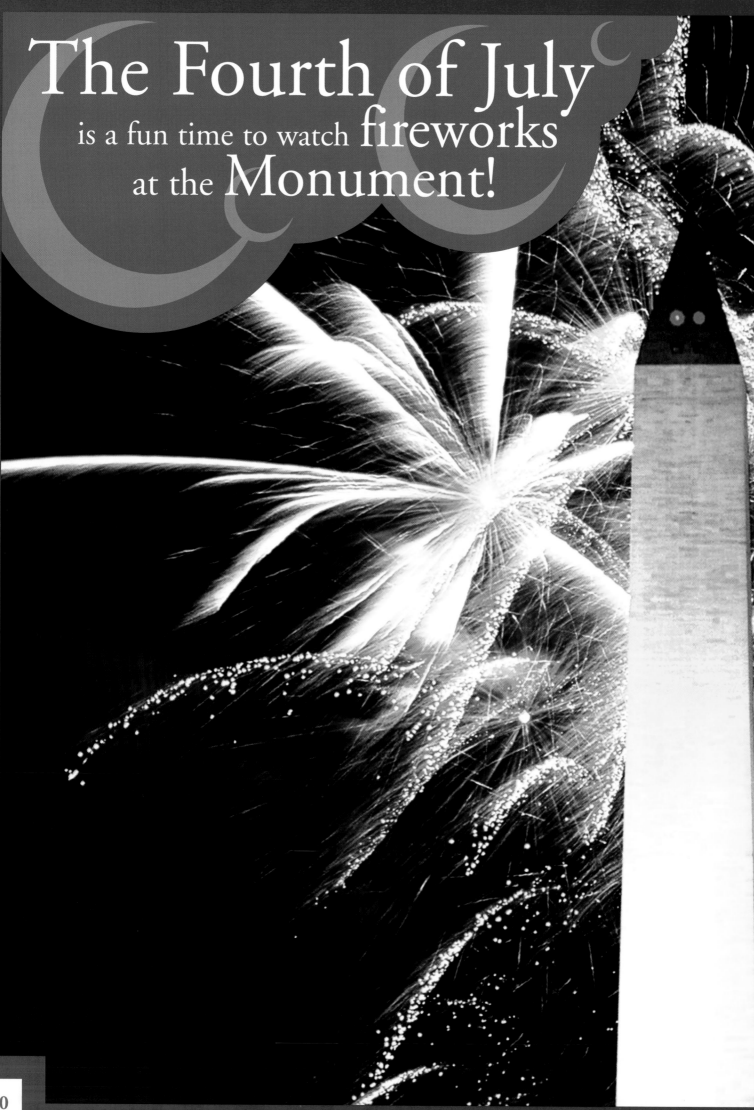

The Fourth of July is a fun time to watch **fireworks** at the **Monument!**

There are two ways to get to the look out points. A person can get their exercise and take the 898 steps up. Are you ready to climb? If you're feeling lazy, you can take the elevator. It's a great view of the city. Even the Blue Ridge Mountains can be seen from up there.

We're now coming to the Lincoln Memorial.

"Say Cheese!"

The Lincoln ★ Memorial

The Lincoln Memorial was opened in 1922 and is one of the most famous buildings around here. It was built to remember our 16th President, Abraham Lincoln. He helped stop slavery and the Civil War. Abe was a patient man. Some people say he was a funny guy too.

Quiet please, and be respectful of others.
This is serious and not a place to run around.

Watch your step please and follow me.
The marble Lincoln statue is 19 feet tall. On the walls, carved in
stone is the Gettysburg Speech that President Lincoln read
in 1863. This Speech honored Civil War soldiers killed
in the Battle of Gettysburg.

The Gettysburg Address says that all men are created equal. This was an important time in America.

"OK!"

"Now we can run around!!"

You look worried, sir!

Don't worry. I see some of you are looking like you need another kind of break. A bathroom break! This is the most important tip of the day. There are many restroom stops. In fact, there is one right below you! In the lower level of the Lincoln Memorial you will find what you're looking for. You'll also see the elevator! So, if you don't want to climb those steps again, you don't have to. Another good bathroom stop is the White House Visitors Center. It is warm and clean. You can even check out historical stuff of the most famous house in the country. You have to go through the metal detectors, so be ready!

Are you tired and hungry yet?

There are lots of places to get food in Washington DC. You can get almost any kind of food at the Smithsonian Museum Cafeterias. The pizza and chicken are delicious. If you want to fill your stomach fast and only have a few dollars, a hotdog can fill you up at any of the street vendors. They like it when you smile at them.

For fancier food, Old Ebbitt Grill, on 15th Street, is a great place for grilled cheese sandwiches. The people are very friendly. Don't forget to bring a friend and leave a nice tip. That's always polite.

Let's take a walk along the Tidal Basin.
The Jefferson Memorial is the round white marble building you can
see right there across the water. Just like the other memorials today,
this was named after an important person in our history.

Thomas Jefferson was an inventor, governor of Virginia and became the 3rd President of the United States in 1801. The Jefferson Memorial was opened to visitors in 1943.

The Jefferson Memorial

TRUTHS TO BE SELF-
ALL MEN ARE CREATED
ARE ENDOWED BY THEIR
CERTAIN INALIENABLE
HESE ARE LIFE, LIBERTY
T OF HAPPINESS, THAT
RIGHTS GOVERNMENTS
AMONG MEN, WE···
H AND DECLARE, THAT
S ARE AND OF RIGH
E AND INDEPEND
THE SUPPORT OF
TH A FIRM REL
CTION OF D
E MUTUALLY PL
FORTUNES AND OU
HONOUR.

Thomas Jefferson wrote the Declaration of Independence at the age of 33. This paper is what made this country separate from England. Without it, we might be talking like Queen Elizabeth! Would you care for a spot of tea, sir?

Want to buy a T-shirt or coffee mug?

You can bargain with the vendor people and maybe even get a two for one sale!

Well, we've come to the end of this tour. Not much rain and pretty good sunshine. I had a great time with you! There are many other things to see in our nation's capital. Come back again for another *Casey Goes to Washington* Tour!

Casey

Lincoln Memorial

23rd Street

20th Street

Rock Creek Parkway

Constitution Avenue

Reflecting Pool

Arlington Memorial Bridge

Independence Avenue

Ohio Drive

POTOMAC RIVER

George Mason Memorial Bridge

National Mall
www.nps.gov/nama

Washington DC Convention &
Tourism Company
www.washington.org

Smithsonian Institution
www.si.edu

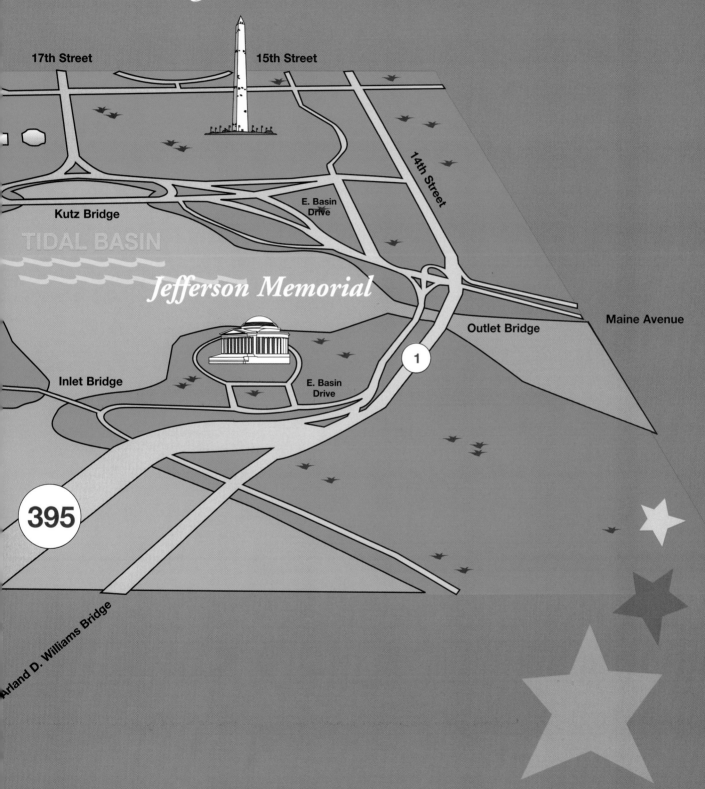

Washington Monument

17th Street

15th Street

14th Street

Kutz Bridge

E. Basin Drive

TIDAL BASIN

Jefferson Memorial

Outlet Bridge

Maine Avenue

1

Inlet Bridge

E. Basin Drive

395

Arland D. Williams Bridge

Arlington National Cemetery
www.arlingtoncemetery.org

Washington Metropolitan Area Transit Authority
www.wmata.com

All About Town Tours
www.allaboutown.com

To My Readers

I hope this book does more than help guide you through our nation's capital, but will help others too. I promise that a special part of your book purchase will go to help many children in Madagascar. Thank you for joining this project.

To learn more about these Madagascar plans and other *Casey Goes To Washington* books, check out my web page at:
www.CaseyBooks.com

Give the Gift of *Casey Goes to Washington* To Your Friends

Check Your Local Bookstore or Order Here

Yes, I want____copies of *Casey Goes to Washington* for $17.95 each (or order 4 at $16 each).

Include $3.95 shipping and handling on one book, and $1.95 for each additional book. Virginia residents must include applicable sales tax.

Payment must accompany orders. Allow 3 weeks for delivery.

My check or money order for $_____ is enclosed.

Please charge my: ◯ Visa ◯ Mastercard ◯ Check*

Name_____

Address_____

City/State/Zip_____

Phone_____ Email_____

Card#_____

Exp. Date_____ Three Digit Code _____

Signature_____

**To order call 703-965-3715
Or detach and mail or fax this form to:**

**Promise Publishing Group
P.O. Box 2221
Reston, Virginia 20195**

Fax: 703-242-2585

*Make your check payable to "Promise Publishing Group"

Look for these Upcoming *Casey Goes to Washington* books!

World War Memorials & *Arlington Cemetery*
FALL 2005

Casey Meets Rolling Thunder
SPRING 2006

Casey Goes to The White House
FALL 2006